AIKEN COLEMAN

INDIAN HOME COOKING

Authentic Recipes and Techniques
from India's Rich Culinary Heritage
(2024 Cookbook)

Copyright © 2023 by Aiken Coleman

All rights reserved. No part of this publication may be reproduced, stored or transmitted in any form or by any means, electronic, mechanical, photocopying, recording, scanning, or otherwise without written permission from the publisher. It is illegal to copy this book, post it to a website, or distribute it by any other means without permission.

First edition

This book was professionally typeset on Reedsy.
Find out more at reedsy.com

Contents

1. Introduction — 1
2. Chapter 01: Understanding the Fundamentals of Indian... — 11
3. Chapter 02: Key Spices in Indian Cuisine and Their... — 25
4. Chapter 03: Breakfast Delights of India — 32
5. Chapter 4: Indian Lunch and Dinner Delights — 47
6. Chapter 05: Indian Sweet Treat Recipes — 64
7. Chapter 06: Vegetarian Indian Delights — 78
8. Conclusion — 85

1

Introduction

India, the vast region in South Asia, boasts one of the world's largest and influential civilizations. It's widely known that Indians have a deep love for food; they enjoy talking about cooking, savoring various dishes, and experimenting with recipes. In every Indian household, there's a unique recipe passed down through generations. However, how much do we truly know about the history of Indian cuisine? This topic delves into the journey of Indian Food Heritage, shedding light on its rich historical background.

Over the course of more than 4,000 years of recorded history, India has welcomed a diverse array of immigrants, each bringing their unique religious traditions. To truly grasp the complexity of India's native culinary culture, one must recognize its remarkable cultural diversity. India is far from a monolithic entity when it comes to food; instead, it's a tapestry woven from various regions and sects, each contributing significantly to the nation's cuisine.

The term "Indian food" is a simplification that an Indian might find amusing, as it's akin to labeling all North American wines under a single category for a wine connoisseur. Across India, countless regions boast their distinct cooking methods, spices, and locally-sourced ingredients. With a population exceeding one billion, India's culinary diversity mirrors its inhabitants' multitude.

The two dominant religious sects in India, Muslims and Hindus, have profoundly influenced the nation's food culture and choices. With each wave of migration, they brought their unique culinary practices. Hindu culture, widespread in vegetarianism, is characterized by its extensive use of rice, and dishes like dosa and idli are prevalent. In contrast, the Muslim culture is renowned for its expertise in meat preparation, offering delicacies such as Mughlai cuisine, kababs, nargisi kaftas, biryani, and tandoor-cooked favorites.

The South Indian cuisine primarily revolves around rice, often accompanied by a light and tangy porridge called Rasam. Coconut plays a vital role in Southern dishes, and steamed rice cakes are highly favored. Beyond this, India's culinary heritage has also been enriched by the contributions of the Portuguese, Persians, and British. The British introduced tea to India, now a beloved beverage.

Indian cuisine can be broadly categorized into four regional types: North, East, South, and West. North India's culinary landscape was significantly influenced by the Mughal dynasty, which ruled for three centuries. Naan bread, commonly associated with Indian cuisine, is actually of Afghan origin and was not a daily staple in India.

In the South, steamed rice cakes are a staple, and rice features prominently in every meal. Coconut is a unifying element in Southern cuisine, and there's a divide between vegetarian and non-vegetarian preferences. Kerala, in particular, is known for its extensive use of coconut in culinary creations.

Western states like Gujarat, Maharashtra, and Goa offer unique culinary experiences. Gujarat's cuisine caters to Muslims, Hindus, Parsis, and Jains, each with their distinct cooking methods. Parsis favor poultry and seafood, while Gujarat is renowned for its vegetarian fare. Maharashtra, with the bustling metropolis of Mumbai, has its own culinary specialties.

Eastern states exhibit distinct characteristics, with Bengali cuisine featuring fish and rice as its cornerstone. It's known for its delicate and subtle flavors. In contrast, Odisha is famous for dishes like deep-fried squash blossoms and rice-based patties. The diet includes cod and other fish, with limited consumption of poultry.

India's culinary diversity is astonishing, with flavors that vary significantly from east to west, yet united by their regional roots and an undeniable sense of boundless taste.

A Concise History of Classic Indian Cuisine

The evolution of Indian cuisine is a tapestry woven with influences from diverse cultures during times of necessity and progression. Some dishes were born out of the need to feed the masses, while others were imported from various regions. Many intriguing stories about these traditional Indian dishes have faded into obscurity. One such example is the tale of Petha.

Petha is older than Taj Mahal:

Petha, a delicacy in Agra, holds significant importance. Its origins are intricately linked to the construction of the Taj Mahal during the Mughal era. As the monumental shrine was being built, around 20,000 workers were growing weary of their monotonous daily meals of dal and roti. Concerned about their well-being, Emperor Shah Jahan sought guidance from the master architect, Ustad Isa Effendi, who turned to Pir Naqshbandi Sahib for a solution. Legend has it that during a moment of deep meditation, Pir Naqshbandi Sahib received divine inspiration and shared the recipe for Petha with the Emperor. Following this revelation, approximately 500 cooks prepared Petha to diversify the workers' meals.

INTRODUCTION

Dal Bati, once a simple meal, became a vital survival resource during wars.:

Dal Bati stands as Rajasthan's finest culinary delight. Its recipe is a story worth telling. This Rajasthani dish finds its origins within the iconic Mewar Chittorgarh Fort. Bati, a crucial component of this dish, consists of wheat dough fried in oil. During challenging wartime conditions, the Mewar Rajput kings relied on Bati as a survival staple. This food could be prepared in the arid desert lands of Rajasthan with minimal supplies and scarce water, making it an essential sustenance option in times of scarcity.

Paraphrase the following text into a completely original, plagiarism-free version in [english]. Maintain the original meaning and approximate length of the text. The output should be a direct paraphrase.

Transformation of Mysore: From Monarchy to Popular Culture:

Mysore, a significant city in South India, has a unique culinary gem known as Mysore Paka, a delectable sweetmeat. Its origin story traces back to the early 20th century within the kitchens of the Mysore Palace. In those days, the royal chef constantly aimed to impress the King with an array of culinary creations. One day, he ingeniously concocted a new sweet dish using chickpea flour, oil, and sugar. When asked about the name of this delectable creation, he spontaneously coined the term 'Mysore Paka,' drawing from the Kannada word 'Paka,' which signifies a sweet mixture. This culinary innovation marked a transition from royal cuisine to becoming a beloved treat in the common culinary landscape.

Khaja: A Culinary Tradition Across Generations in Mauryan and Gupta Eras

The art of making Khaja is a cherished tradition for the people of Orissa. Historically, this culinary technique is believed to have been borrowed from the central highlands of Bihar approximately 2200 years ago. The origins of Khaja can be traced back to the ancient Indian Gupta empires. Rajgir's Khaja in Bihar is renowned for its delightful puffiness, while Kakinada's Khaja in Andhra Pradesh is celebrated for its crisp exterior and savory interior. This sweet treat has stood the test of time, passing down through generations, preserving the culinary heritage of the Mauryan and Gupta realms.

Jalebi's Origin Is Not Strictly Indian:

Jalebi, a renowned sweet dish in India, has its origins traced back to West Asia. The introduction of Jalebi to India occurred during medieval times when Persian-speaking invaders brought this sweet treat. In the 14th century, it was referred to as 'Kundalika' and 'Jalavallika' in India. Interestingly, during Ramadan in Iran, Jalebi was generously served to the less fortunate.

Dum Biryani: A Lifeline for the Needy in Awadh

Historical accounts reveal that biryani finds its origins in Hyderabad, the provincial capital, during the Nawab period. Some discussions suggest its inception in the early medieval era during Timur's invasion of India. Amidst these debates, Dum Biryani, also known as Awadh's Biryani, surfaced in Lucknow. In times of scarcity, the Nawab of Awadh instructed the impoverished residents to prepare meals in large handis (round-shaped brass pots). These pots were sealed, and food was cooked in substantial quantities with minimal energy, a technique known as 'dum.' This culinary practice served as a vital source of sustenance for the needy in the region.

The Popularity of Indian Cuisine in the United States

Indian food is rapidly gaining popularity in the United States, becoming a highly specialized and sought-after culinary choice. Besides Chinese cuisine, which has already integrated into American dining, Indian culinary influences are becoming increasingly prominent on food networks and restaurant menus across the country. The delectable taste of Indian dishes has earned them worldwide acclaim, leading to the proliferation of Indian restaurants globally, especially in the US.

These restaurants offer a diverse range of salads, appetizers, sweets, side dishes, and desserts, catering to a broad audience. Indian cuisine's appeal lies in its rich variety of spices and aromatic flavors, captivating the taste buds of diners. The culinary techniques, unique to different regions of India, have been introduced to the Western world, gaining immense popularity among citizens. Special occasions are marked with the preparation of distinct dishes, showcasing the culinary artistry of Indian chefs.

India's position as the world's largest fruit supplier highlights its vast agricultural potential. Additionally, the country possesses significant scientific and engineering expertise, which is being harnessed to create modern, popular food products in the US market. The demand for new Indian products continues to grow, particularly in the US, where people have developed a fondness for Indian cuisine.

Indian spices are renowned not only for their flavor but also for their therapeutic benefits. Common herbs like turmeric, ginger, and cardamom are widely used due to their medicinal properties. Americans are particularly inclined towards Indian food because of these health benefits associated with the spices. Many individuals believe that consuming Indian food does not harm their bodies; instead, the medicinal properties of the spices enhance their well-being.

In Washington DC, numerous Indian restaurants prepare mouth-watering dishes, serving both locals and visitors. Each eatery showcases its unique culinary art, contributing to the diverse food culture in the region. International buyers have been captivated by the array of spices and ingredients used in Indian cooking.

This growing fascination with Indian cuisine and its spices has led to the publication of various resources, including books detailing Indian culinary traditions. In such publications, readers can explore Indian cuisine, delve into the intricacies of commonly used spices, and find a wealth of recipes, enabling them to savor the rich flavors of Indian cooking in their own homes.

2

Chapter 01: Understanding the Fundamentals of Indian Gastronomy

The culinary landscape of India encompasses a rich tapestry of both contemporary and traditional cuisines from the Indian subcontinent. Due to the diverse geographical features, climates, historical influences, ethnic diversity, and occupations, these cuisines vary significantly, utilizing locally sourced herbs, vegetables, and fruits. Moreover, Indian cuisine is deeply intertwined with religious practices, especially Hinduism, as well as societal choices and rituals.

1.1 Overview of Regional Indian Cuisines

Although Indian restaurants often present dishes in a standardized nationalized manner, the reality is that India's culinary landscape is as diverse and unique as its people. These regional foods are profoundly influenced by India's past, its trade relationships, as well as its cultural and religious traditions. Understanding the commonalities and variations among India's regional cuisines can elevate your next Indian dining experience into an engaging and deeply satisfying culinary adventure.

While Indian cuisine boasts distinct regional uniqueness, there are shared elements that tie together the diverse culinary practices across the country. Sauces play a pivotal role in Indian cooking, serving as the base for a variety of dishes, whether they are sauce-like or soup-like, featuring meats, potatoes, or cheese. However, the specific spice blends, consistency, and ingredients are determined by regional preferences. Agriculture plays a fundamental role in Indian cuisine, with Southern Indian regions relying more heavily on rice than other areas. Legumes or "pulses" are essential ingredients in both regional cuisines. Indian cooking incorporates a wide variety of peas, including red lentils, black gram, peas, yellow gram, black gram, and green gram, which are used whole, broken, or ground into flour. These legumes not only add texture but also provide a source of tartness to dishes, making them suitable for vegan diets.

One of the most distinctive features of Indian cuisine is its rich and varied use of spices. Indian spice blends typically incorporate up to five different spices, sometimes even more. Garam masala, a popular spice mixture, includes cardamom, cinnamon, and clove, with the specific spices used varying by region and personal recipe. This intricate interplay of spices is what gives Indian food its unique and tantalizing flavors.

Within India's culinary tapestry, the influence of trade and historical conquests is unmistakable. Various regions and dishes bear the imprint of international interactions. Arab and Canadian traders coveted India's spices, leading to a reciprocal exchange that left a lasting mark on Indian gastronomy. Portuguese merchants introduced New World ingredients like onions, peppers, and chilies, which seamlessly melded into Indian cuisine. Additionally, Arab traders brought coffee to India.

The period of foreign rule also significantly impacted Indian culinary traditions. The Mughal rulers, reigning over India from the early 1500s to the late 1600s, introduced Persian spices and culinary practices. This influence is evident in the use of cheese and milk in sauces, the inclusion of meat and nuts in salads, and the development of particular salad preparations.

While the British presence in India introduced the nation to tea and soup, it had minimal effect on Indian cuisine. However, the assimilation of Indian food into British society had a profound influence on the international perception of Indian cuisine. Tikka Masala, a flavorful sauce frequently found on Indian menus, was originally an Anglo-Indian creation and is often referred to as "Britain's true national dish." Even European interpretations of Indian "curry," encompassing a wide range of garlicky and stew-like dishes, are rooted in the British understanding of Indian cooking.

India: A Diverse Nation

India's population is incredibly diverse, with cultural traditions deeply molded by ethnic and religious distinctions. Ayurvedic principles have also played a role in shaping Indian cuisine, emphasizing the harmonious balance between mind, body, and spirit through spice combinations and cooking techniques. This philosophy exerts a profound influence on Indian cooking, shaped by religious and cultural characteristics.

Approximately one-third of India's population follows a vegetarian diet, largely influenced by Hindu, Jain, or Buddhist beliefs. Consequently, a significant portion of the country's cuisine abstains from beef. Religious traditions also dictate other dietary restrictions; Hindus avoid beef due to the sacred nature of cattle, while Muslims abstain from pork as they consider it impure. The ingredients used in cooking can vary according to the dominant religious beliefs in a particular region.

Northern Indian Cuisine

Northern Indian cuisine, perhaps the most widely recognized Indian culinary style outside of India, prominently features Mughal influences. It is characterized by a high consumption of dairy products, including milk, paneer (a mild Indian cheese), butter, and yogurt. Well-known Northern Indian treats include samosas and, on occasion, beef. Tandoors, clay ovens, are commonly used in the North, imparting a unique barbecue flavor to dishes like naan. Many popular Northern dishes regularly appear on Indian menus, such as Dal or Paneer Makhani, which are vegetarian dishes featuring dal or paneer cooked in a creamy tomato sauce with onions, mango powder, and curry spices. Korma, another Northern Indian staple, is a creamy curry made with coconut milk or yogurt, along with cumin, cilantro, and a small amount of cashews or walnuts. It can be paired with various meats, typically poultry or lamb, but sometimes beef, as well as a vegetarian option with paneer.

Western Indian Cuisine

The culinary traditions of Western India are shaped by the region's political and cultural peculiarities. The coastal region of Maharashtra is known for its milk-centric seafood and coconut-based dishes. Gujarati cuisine is predominantly vegetarian and has a subtle sweetness in most of its preparations due to strong regional influences. This region's arid climate has led to a focus on chutneys, a common Indian condiment featuring fried, fresh, or pickled fruits and vegetables with sweet, sour, or spicy flavors. Goa, which served as a significant port and Portuguese colony, boasts a unique fusion of Indian and Portuguese culinary elements. Goan cuisine incorporates beef and pork more liberally than other Indian cuisines. The use of vinegar is a distinguishing feature of Goan dishes, and the coastal setting ensures the prevalence of coconut milk, coconut powder, and fish in Goan cuisine.

Eastern Indian Cuisine

The cuisine of Eastern India is renowned for its sweets, which are not only popular within the region but also found in restaurants. These delicate desserts provide a delightful conclusion to any meal. A common sweet treat is Rasgulla, featuring balls made from semolina and cheese curd boiled in a light sugar syrup. Eastern dishes often incorporate mustard seeds and mustard oil, imparting a distinct aroma to the food. Rice and seafood are also prominent in Eastern cuisine, which tends to be spicier compared to many other regions of India.

Southern Indian Cuisine

Southern Indian cuisine is less commonly featured on restaurant menus and differs significantly from other regions. Their "curries" exhibit a wide range of textures, ranging from drier preparations to those with a stew-like or soupy consistency. Poriyals, dry curries comprising a medley of vegetables and seasonings, complement rice-based meals. Sambars, essentially pea and vegetable stews with a tamarind flavor, have a soupier quality compared to curries from other regions but are smoother than rasams. Rasams, similar to soups, primarily consist of tomatoes, tamarind, and various spices. Kootus, resembling curries from other regions, derive their thickness from lentils rather than dairy, in contrast to the North's dairy-rich curries.

Southern Indian cuisine is renowned for its delectable fried or griddle-cooked sweets, alongside curry-style dishes. Dosas, large crepe-like pancakes, are typically served with vegetable curries or chutneys. Idli, a savory doughnut-like delicacy, pairs perfectly with sambar and rasam. Apart from restaurants specializing in Southern Indian cuisine, pappadams, crisp rice cookies seasoned with black peppercorns, are the most commonly encountered South Indian food items in Indian restaurants.

1.2 Characteristics of Indian Cuisine

Indian cuisine has transcended international borders and gained global recognition. Dishes like Tandoori chicken, Pav bhaji, and Kesar kulfi are beloved worldwide. Food enthusiasts everywhere appreciate both vegetarian and non-vegetarian Indian delicacies.

Current Trend

An increasing number of patrons are flocking to renowned Indian restaurants worldwide to savor popular Indian culinary delights. Indian cuisine is experiencing rapid growth in the global food industry. Tandoori dishes, in particular, are in high demand globally. North Indian cuisine is exceptionally delectable, offering a wide array of tantalizing options such as Tandoori Chicken, Chicken Reshmi Kebabs, and much more.

Diverse Abundance

The exceptional diversity of Indian food has contributed to its growing popularity. Indian cuisine caters to a wide range of tastes, satisfying various palates. Some individuals are captivated by the flavors of South Indian delicacies, while others are enamored with Punjabi, Rajasthani, Goan, Parsi, or delectable Bengali dishes. The realm of Indian street food has been revitalized through innovative fusion variations.

Unstoppable Culinary Creativity

Most Indian dishes are prepared in a manner that preserves the nutritional value of ingredients, ensuring that the cooking process does not compromise their health benefits. Indian cuisine derives its authentic taste from a myriad of spices, many of which are beneficial for the skin. Different regions in India offer unique pickles and greens, each with distinct flavors that can tantalize your taste buds.

1.3 Importance of Including Indian Foods in Your Diet and Their Advantages

Considering various factors, we have compiled a list of essential Indian foods that should be a part of everyone's diet. It's important to consult your doctor if you have any health conditions to determine what foods are suitable for you based on this list.

Fruits

A variety of fruits from the Indian heritage are highly beneficial for your health. They are rich in vital vitamins and minerals necessary for our well-being. Include seasonal and yearly fruits such as strawberries, bananas, pomegranates, and pineapples in your daily diet. While some individuals with specific health issues might need to avoid certain fruits, these fruits are generally excellent healthy options, replacing unhealthy snacks like fried chips. Benefits of consuming fruits include:

- Fruits supply essential nutrients like calcium, dietary fiber, and vitamin C, often lacking in our diets.
    - Most fruits are low in sugar, salt, and calories.
    - Fruit consumption provides quick energy, making it an ideal snack for busy schedules.
    - The fiber in fruits not only aids digestion but also contributes to a feeling of fullness when combined with proteins in your diet.

Chilies

Fresh chilies, particularly rich in vitamin C, are excellent for your health, especially if you enjoy spicy food. There are milder chili options available for those who prefer less intense spiciness, offering the same benefits without the burning sensation. Chilies also boost metabolism. Benefits of consuming chilies include:

- Chilies contain up to seven times the vitamin C found in oranges, providing various health benefits such as reducing sinus inflammation, boosting metabolism, relieving migraines, and alleviating heart, joint, and nerve pain.
    - Chilies have historically been used to prevent food contamination and are considered a potential metabolic accelerator aiding in weight loss.
    - They might contribute to managing leukemia and preventing lung cancer.

Beans

Beans are an excellent source of protein, calcium, magnesium, and folic acid. They are versatile and can be used in various Indian dishes. Moreover, they are commonly used in cuisines worldwide, from Asia to the USA. Benefits of consuming beans include:

- Beans are heart-healthy as they contain soluble fiber, which helps reduce cholesterol levels.
    - Most beans are low in fat (around 2 to 3%) and do not contribute to cholesterol, unless prepared with other high-fat ingredients.
    - Rich in fiber, beans promote regularity and prevent acid reflux.
    - Consuming beans regularly can lower the risk of cardiovascular diseases.

Garlic

Garlic, renowned for its savory taste, is also celebrated for its medicinal properties. It serves as a natural source of antimicrobial agents. Key benefits of garlic include the production of Allicin, a compound with powerful healing properties. Regular consumption, either raw or in the diet, reduces total cholesterol due to Allicin's antioxidant nature. The stimulating properties of garlic protect the body from free radicals, slowing down collagen depletion, which leads to aging skin losing its vitality.

Spices

Indian spices, known globally since ancient times for their incredible flavors, also offer remarkable health benefits. Turmeric, or Haldi, has soothing qualities, lowers cholesterol, and prevents blood clots, reducing the risk of heart attacks. Cardamom boosts metabolism, while the ingredients in garam masala aid digestion due to their varied nutrient levels. Nutritional benefits of spices include:

- Many herbs and spices provide more antioxidants than fruits and vegetables, boosting disease resistance.
    - Cinnamon exhibits potent anti-diabetic properties, reducing blood sugar levels.
    - Turmeric contains curcumin, a substance with significant antioxidant effects.
    - Ginger has anti-inflammatory properties and can alleviate nausea.

Paneer

Paneer, a staple in vegetarian diets but also consumed by non-vegetarians, is versatile and can be incorporated into various dishes. Homemade paneer made from milk produces fewer fatty acids and cholesterol, making it a healthier option. Paneer offers:

- Rich protein source, especially beneficial for vegetarian diets lacking meat intake.
    - Steady energy release into the bloodstream due to its protein content, preventing blood sugar spikes.
    - High in linoleic acid, a fatty acid that aids weight loss by enhancing the body's fat-burning mechanism.
    - Prevents various health issues such as osteoporosis, knee discomfort, tooth decay, and gum problems.

Flour and Rice

White rice, widely consumed in India, can be substituted with brown rice, which is higher in protein, making it a healthier choice. Switching to whole wheat flour, also applicable to other wheat products like bread, is becoming increasingly popular. Rice and flour provide:

- Insoluble fibers essential for eliminating waste and combating constipation when combined with foods like nuts, beans, and cabbage.
    - High protein content and abundant B vitamins.
    - Dietary fiber, vital for digestion, found in rice, aiding the movement of waste products through the digestive tract.

Pulses

Pulses are a significant part of the Indian diet, rich in nutritious fibers, vitamins A, B, C, and E, as well as minerals like calcium and iron. They are a primary nutrition source in vegetarian diets and offer:

- Reduced risk of heart disease with increased consumption of pulses.
    - Low sugar content, making them favorable for regulating blood sugar levels.
    - Affordable and healthy protein source.

Leafy Vegetables

Green leafy vegetables are already a common inclusion in the Indian diet, with options like spinach and cabbages available throughout the year. Leafy greens offer:

- Cholesterol-lowering properties in mustard and kale greens.
    - Improved vision and reduced risk of cataracts, providing essential nutrients and energy.

- Elevated calcium levels, giving them a slightly acidic taste.

Eggs

While not suitable for vegetarian diets, eggs are excellent sources of high-quality protein. While the yolk contains cholesterol, incorporating egg whites provides essential minerals and nutrients. Eggs offer:

- High-quality protein source, beneficial for all age groups.
    - Consumption during childhood, coupled with reduced sugary intake, contributes to healthy growth.
    - Despite cholesterol content, eggs do not adversely affect blood cholesterol levels.
    - Rich in nutrients supporting heart health.

1.4 Health Benefits of Incorporating Indian Cuisine

Utilizing spices like onions, turmeric, ginger, and garlic in cooking contributes to numerous health benefits, including improved cholesterol levels, reduced cancer risk, and enhanced kidney function. While it's common knowledge that Indian cuisine offers various health advantages due to its use of spices and vegetables, what might surprise you is that Indian food isn't just flavorful but also healthful. Most Indian dishes are plant-based, and research indicates the positive impacts of a plant-based diet. Here are some of these benefits:

A Nutrient-Rich Vegetarian Diet

Indian meals comprise a variety of nutritious ingredients such as vegetables, legumes, and grains. The combination of rice provides complete proteins, ensuring a balanced diet. Since Indian cuisine incorporates diverse foods daily, it maximizes the intake of different minerals and vitamins from various plants. The vegetables in these dishes contain nutrients and antioxidants beneficial for overall health, liver, and brain. Sulphur compounds present in ingredients like garlic, cauliflower, and cabbage aid in detoxifying the body from mycotoxins and harmful toxins.

Anti-Inflammatory Effects

Spices like turmeric possess anti-inflammatory properties, reducing the risk of various chronic diseases. They are effective in alleviating inflammation. Other spices not only decrease inflammation but also enhance metabolism, assist in weight management, and aid in detoxifying the body. Cinnamon, for example, helps regulate blood sugar levels. If you enjoy spicy Indian cuisine, chili peppers are your allies, not only enhancing flavor but also contributing to your overall health. Chilies are rich in vitamin C and vitamin A.

Rich in Dietary Fiber

Indian cuisine incorporates good sources of both soluble and insoluble fibers, including chickpeas, green vegetables, corn, lentils, and green beans. When these fibers come into contact with water, soluble fibers from peas and beans form a gel-like substance, significantly reducing cholesterol levels and regulating blood sugar. Insoluble dietary fiber promotes regular bowel movements and prevents indigestion.

Benefits of Ghee

Ghee, when used in moderation, is nutritious and possesses healing properties. Pure cow ghee plays a vital role in Indian and Ayurvedic medicinal cooking. It serves as a healthier alternative to butter, palm oil, and various processed fats available in the market. Ghee's molecular structure is more stable than olive oil, and it doesn't quickly spoil or become rancid. Many vegetable oils in the market break down during heating, leading to oxidation and the production of harmful free radicals in the body. Ghee protects against toxins, supplies essential fatty acids crucial for hormone development, reduces inflammation, aids in nutrient absorption, and enhances metabolism according to Ayurvedic principles.

1.5 Differences Between Home-Cooked Indian Food and Restaurant Cuisine

South Asian cuisine is known for its rich, flavorful, and satisfying dishes, making it an integral part of the lives of many USA-Asians, whether enjoyed at home or in local restaurants. However, there are distinct differences between the two dining experiences, shaped by cultural preferences and generational shifts within the community.

In the past, South Asians in the USA rarely dined out, considering it an unnecessary luxury and often distrusting the authenticity of 'outside' cuisine. Dining out was not a common practice, especially among extended families living together, where meals were typically prepared at home. Today, younger generations of USA-Asians are more inclined to dine out, appreciating the social and enjoyable aspects of restaurant meals, while also valuing the unique flavors of home-cooked food.

Home-cooked Indian food holds a special place for many USA Asians due to its personalized nature, allowing for the inclusion of favorite ingredients and family recipes. The freedom to experiment with flavors and incorporate cherished elements like special herbs, achaar (pickles), or yogurt is a unique aspect of home cooking. Despite the time and effort required, cooking at home is seen as an expression of love and care for the family.

Restaurant dining, on the other hand, offers a wide variety of dishes, allowing individuals to choose from an extensive menu. It provides a convenient option for social gatherings and allows people to indulge in a diverse selection of dishes, such as the popular restaurant item Chicken Tikka Masala. While restaurant portions may seem limited to those with hearty appetites, the flexibility of adding more food, if needed, is an advantage of home-cooked meals.

However, the modern lifestyle, characterized by fast-paced routines, has led to a growing preference for eating out among younger individuals. The convenience of restaurant dining appeals to those with hectic lives, despite the enduring appeal of traditional home-cooked meals among older generations.

In summary, the choice between home-cooked Indian food and restaurant cuisine is a matter of personal preference and convenience. While both options have their merits, the love and attention invested in home-cooked meals make them a cherished tradition, even in the face of changing dining habits.

3

Chapter 02: Key Spices in Indian Cuisine and Their Characteristics

Indian cuisine is renowned for its extensive use of diverse spices, which are skillfully blended and utilized in a wide array of recipes. The same spice can yield entirely distinct flavors through subtle variations in cooking techniques. To explore these incredible ingredients, we have identified several of the most commonly used spices in India, each contributing to the rich tapestry of Indian flavors.

Red Chili Powder

Red chili powder is derived from red chili seeds and is incredibly potent, serving as the spiciest element of chili. It should be used sparingly due to its intense heat. Introduced to India by Americans and Portuguese, it has become a crucial component of Indian cuisine, enhancing various Southern Indian curries. The defining characteristic of chili powder is its heat, likely due to its capsaicin content, although some varieties also offer distinct fragrance and flavor.

Mustard Seeds

Brown mustard seeds are widely utilized in Indian cooking. They can be roasted whole to flavor oil, which is then used in raw food preparation. This flavorful oil doubles as a dipping sauce. Though native to Rome, a comparable usage is found in Buddhist literature, where certain seeds are used to save a child's life.

Coriander

Coriander, part of the Parsley Genus, produces round, ridged seeds that transition from dark green to bright orange as they mature. This spice boasts a tangy, pleasant flavor with a mild citrusy aroma. Coriander, one of the world's oldest spices, is commonly cultivated in the Rajasthan States.

Cinnamon

Cinnamon, with its sweet taste and soft, woody fragrance, is ideal for desserts and cakes. It not only adds spice but also offers health benefits, such as lowering cholesterol and combating leukemia. Primarily grown along the Western Ghats of Kerala and Tamil Nadu, it enriches the cuisines of these regions.

Asafoetida

Asafoetida, a resin derived from a plant's base, possesses a pungent, garlic-like sulfur scent in its natural state. When cooked in oil, its aroma diminishes, and its flavor improves significantly. Often added to boiling oil before other ingredients, it is valued for its truffle-like taste and roasted garlic aroma. Grown primarily in Kashmir and parts of Punjab, it is known for its anti-flatulence properties.

Cumin

Cumin, extracted from the Parsley group, imparts a smoky flavor and strong fragrance to most Indian sauces and vegetables. The seeds are dry-roasted and ground before use and are the first spice added in Indian cooking. Careful usage is necessary as it burns quickly and can become overpowering.

Saffron

Saffron, the world's most expensive spice, originates from Kashmir and is obtained from Crocus Bulbs. Its musky, honey-like scent is its most notable feature. Commonly soaked in water or milk to mellow its intense fragrance and taste, it is a prized ingredient in various dishes.

Turmeric

Turmeric, belonging to the ginger family, is extensively used in India. It has been used as a pigment for centuries and has diverse applications in traditional Ayurvedic medicine. Derived from the roots of the Indian plant Curcuma Longa, it possesses an earthy quality and a mild aroma. Used in cooking and skincare products, it has medicinal properties, aiding in skin issues and diabetes management.

Cardamom

Cardamom, the world's third most expensive spice, is valued for its strong taste and scent. While green cardamom has a mild eucalyptus color and taste, black cardamom is smoky and often used for its seeds. Widely used in Indian and other sweet dishes, it enhances the flavor and aroma. It also serves medicinal purposes, combating bad breath and stomach diseases. Chewing whole cardamom is beneficial for managing diabetes.

Indian Bay Leaf

Distinct from European Bay Leaf, Indian Bay Leaf belongs to the Lauraceae family and comes from a cinnamon tree parent. It has white streaks on its leaves and imparts a strong spice taste. Found in northern India, the Himalayan slopes, and Nepal, it is critical in Mughal cuisine, enhancing popular dishes like Korma and biryani.

Ginger

Ginger stands as one of India's most valuable crops, yielding over a thousand tonnes annually. Fresh ginger is the primary form used, with dried ginger being limited to specific states such as Goa and Kashmir. There are two major types of ginger: "Cochin," transported from southern Kerala, and "Calicut," from northern Kerala. Both varieties are highly aromatic, containing about 4 percent essential oil and low fiber content. Indian ginger is favored for its milder, more nuanced taste compared to ginger from other countries. In Indian cuisine, fresh ginger is more prevalent than its dried counterpart.

Curry Leaves

Curry leaves, despite their name, don't contribute spice but come from a bush in the Rutaceae family native to India and Sri Lanka. The curry tree is now grown across India, especially in the southern regions. Many households cultivate it in their gardens due to its ease of growth. The leaves are utilized in northern Indian dishes, often paired with ingredients like potatoes and peas in samosa stuffing, as well as in sauces for beef and poultry.

Kalonji/Nigella

Kalonji, also known as black cumin, features black triangular seeds with a mild, somewhat bitter taste, coupled with earthy tones and an onion-like pungency. India is the leading producer of Kalonji, with Egypt and Morocco being other significant sources. These seeds possess potent antioxidant properties and are associated with various medicinal benefits, including combating asthma, fever, pneumonia, and other fall-related illnesses.

Ajowan

Ajowan, another seed spice from the Umbelliferae family, has a faint bitter earthy flavor and a fragrance similar to thyme but more intense. Cooking, especially baking, tempers its impact, resulting in a distinctive nutty taste. Rajasthan is the leading producer of Ajowan in India, contributing to 90 percent of the total production. It's used in savory snacks and baked goods in Indian cuisine, adding a savory touch to vegetable dishes. Ajowan is valued for its therapeutic properties, aiding digestion, curing colds, and reducing bloating.

Dark Brown Mustard

Dark brown mustard, popular in flavor-rich countries like Indonesia and India, is widely used in European and American cuisines to produce mustard sauce. There are three types: light, brown, and black, with the latter two being pungent. In North-Eastern India, a unique mustard sauce is prepared by soaking mustard seeds for several days. Mustard seeds develop their pungency when ground or crushed, combined with a liquid, and stabilized with an acidic substance.

Fenugreek

Fenugreek, belonging to the Legumes family, is used in fresh, dry, and seed forms. Its flavor is a unique blend of bitterness and sourness, with toasting reducing the bitterness. Widely used in Indian and Turkish cuisine, fenugreek seeds are essential in curries, complementing the flavor of vegetables like pumpkin in Punjab and enhancing dosa in Southern India. It's also a component of the Bengali five-spice blend. Beyond culinary use, fenugreek aids in digestion, manages colitis, and enhances milk supply for breastfeeding mothers.

Clove

Clove, a spice derived from the crisped unopened buds of a vine in the Myrtle family, originated in the Moluccas island chains. Clove production extended to Indonesia and Tanzania, with Sri Lanka being a significant supplier to South India. Clove is primarily used in Indian cooking for spice blends and masalas due to its strong fragrance and flavor. It has a high proportion of volatile oil, making even a small quantity impactful. Clove is renowned for its antioxidant properties.

Black Pepper

Black pepper, produced from Piper nigrum plant berries, comes in three main varieties: white, black, and green pepper. Native to the Malabar region in southern India, black pepper is also cultivated in Kerala. The drying process, involving oxidation, results in black pepper, which is extensively used in spice mixes and meat and chicken dishes in northern India.

Amchur Powder

Amchur powder, a sweet and malty spice, serves as a thickening agent and imparts a sour fruity taste to curries, sauces, and chutneys. Beyond its culinary use, it adds unique flavors to a variety of dishes.

4

Chapter 03: Breakfast Delights of India

In this chapter, we present a delightful collection of Indian breakfast recipes that are not only delicious but also designed to fit into your busy morning routine. Whether you prefer the hearty flavors of Northern India or the light and zesty delights of the South, this chapter has something for everyone. These recipes are carefully curated to save you time without compromising on taste, making them perfect for your busy mornings.

Explore the culinary wonders of both Northern and Southern India, all within the confines of your kitchen. With easy-to-follow recipes scattered throughout this chapter, you can now whip up a variety of traditional Indian breakfast and brunch dishes in a matter of minutes. Embrace the flavors, savor the aromas, and enjoy the satisfaction of creating these culinary masterpieces right in your own home. Get ready to transform your mornings with these quick and convenient Indian breakfast recipes!

CHAPTER 03: BREAKFAST DELIGHTS OF INDIA

Vegetable Semolina Upma

Preparation Time: 20 minutes
Serves: 2

Ingredients:
- 1 cup semolina (Rava)
- 1 onion, sliced
- ¼ cup peas
- 1 cup assorted diced vegetables
- 3 green chilies, sliced
- 1 tablespoon sliced ginger
- A few curry leaves
- ½ teaspoon urad dal
- ¼ teaspoon mustard seeds
- Sliced coriander leaves for garnish

- 1 tablespoon oil
- Salt to taste

Method:

1. Heat oil in a large saucepan over medium-high heat.
2. Add finely chopped seeds, red chilies, and ginger. Blend well using a wooden skewer.
3. Add peas and dal, stir to combine, cover the pan tightly and cook for a few minutes.
4. Meanwhile, chop all the vegetables individually. Add them to the pan and mix well.
5. Pour enough water, add salt, cover the pan, and cook over medium-high heat until a thick mixture forms.
6. In a non-stick pan, heat 1 tablespoon of oil and roast semolina over medium-high heat for a couple of minutes.
7. When the vegetables are cooked, gradually add the cooked semolina, stirring constantly to avoid lumps.
8. Cook on low flame for 5 minutes, transfer to a serving bowl, and garnish with cashews and mint leaves.
9. Serve hot.

Semolina Upma with Coconut

Preparation Time: 30 minutes
Serves: 4 persons

Ingredients:
- 1 cup semolina (sooji)
- 2 teaspoons ghee
- 1 ½ teaspoons mustard seeds
- Asafetida to taste

- 10 split organic cashews
- 1 teaspoon Chana dal and urad dal (soaked for 10 minutes)
- 1 tablespoon diced ginger
- 1 small red onion, sliced
- 1 green chili, diced
- 10 curry leaves
- 4 tablespoons green peas
- 2.5 cups water
- Salt to taste
- 2 teaspoons minced cilantro
- 1 teaspoon ghee

Method:

1. Roast the sooji over medium heat until moist, stirring continuously for about 5 minutes. Transfer to another dish.
2. This step can be done in advance for busy mornings.
3. Heat 2 tablespoons of oil in the same pan over medium heat.
4. Add seeds, asafetida, cashews, soaked dal, and ginger. Stir fry for 1 minute until they begin to change color.
5. Add carrot, green chili, and curry leaves. Cook for an additional minute after adding onions.
6. Add peas and stir until the fresh aroma of peas emerges.
7. Pour in 3 cups of water, add lemon zest, and cilantro. Mix well. For a touch of sweetness, honey or sugar can be added.
8. Bring the water to a boil. Gradually add the cooked sooji while stirring continuously with a dough scraper.
9. Cover the pot and simmer on low heat for some time.
10. Remove the lid, add 2 teaspoons of ghee (optional but recommended). Turn off the heat.
11. Serve the Upma warm with coconut chutney.

Puffed Rice Upma

Serves: 1-2 persons
Cooking time: 15 minutes

Ingredients:
- 3 cups puffed rice
- 1 small onion, finely chopped
- 1 small tomato, finely chopped
- 1-2 green chilies, finely chopped
- ½ teaspoon turmeric powder
- ½ teaspoon mustard seeds
- 1 dry red chili, sliced
- A few curry leaves
- 2 teaspoons oil
- Salt to taste

Method:

1. Chop all the ingredients.
2. Heat a skillet with one tablespoon of oil. Add mustard seeds.
3. Add dry red chili and urad dal to the seeds. Fry until the dal turns brown.
4. Add all the chopped ingredients.
5. Also, add salt and turmeric. Cover and let it cook for a minute.
6. Rinse the puffed rice with running water to remove excess moisture. Squeeze out water and quickly return it to the pan.
7. Add it to the pan and cook over high heat for a moment.
8. Remove from heat.
9. Serve the puffed rice upma immediately.

Note:

- Do not wash the puffed rice, as it will become soggy.
- Puffed rice upma is best enjoyed while moist.

Tamarind and Semolina Upma

Cooking time: 20-30 minutes
Serves: 6-8 people

Ingredients:
- 2 cups semolina (Rava)
- 1 thinly chopped onion
- 3-4 green chilies, chopped
- ½ cup roughly chopped ginger
- 1 cup minced vegetables
- 1 ½ teaspoons ghee
- 9 cashew nuts (optional)
- 4 cups water
- Salt

Seasoning:
- 1 teaspoon mustard seeds
- 1 sprig curry leaves
- 1 teaspoon cumin seeds
- 1 teaspoon Bengal gram
- 1 teaspoon black gram

Method:

1. Heat oil in a pan, add cumin and mustard seeds.
2. Add curry leaves, onion, and green chilies. Cook until they change color.
3. Add Bengal gram and fry until it turns golden.

4. Pour in water, add salt, and bring it to a boil.
5. Add semolina gradually while stirring constantly.
6. Cover and cook over medium-high heat until all moisture is absorbed.
7. Reduce the heat and steam until cooked.
8. Turn off the heat and serve.

Ragi Idli

Servings: 4 persons

Ingredients:
- 1 cup idli rice
- 2 cups ragi flour
- 1 cup dal
- ½ teaspoon fenugreek seeds
- Salt to taste

Steps:

1. Soak dal, fenugreek seeds, and ragi separately for 4 hours. Clean and rinse rice independently.
2. Blend dal and seeds until smooth. Set aside.
3. Crush rice into a coarse flour, add water to make a rough batter.
4. Mix rice batter into dal-seed mixture. Add salt and blend well.
5. Let the batter ferment until it reaches the consistency of idli batter.
6. Steam the batter in idli molds for 20 minutes or until a toothpick comes out clean.
7. Serve hot with chutney.

Rava Idli with Sabudana

Cook Time: 12 minutes
Servings: 15

Ingredients:
- 1 cup semolina (sooji)
- 1 tablespoon mustard seeds
- 1 teaspoon cumin seeds
- 1 tablespoon Chana dal
- 1 tablespoon black gram dal (split)
- 1/3 cup sliced cashew nuts
- 1 sprig shredded curry leaves
- 1 tablespoon ginger, chopped
- Asafoetida to taste
- 2 chilies, chopped
- Oil
- 2 tablespoons thinly sliced coriander leaves
- Salt
- ¼ cup tapioca pearls
- 1 cup yogurt, beaten
- Oil for greasing

Method:

1. Boil tapioca pearls in water for two hours, drain, and squeeze out excess water.
2. Heat oil in a pan. Add mustard seeds and let them splutter. Add cumin seeds and dal mixture. Cook until golden.
3. Add asafoetida, curry leaves, ginger, and chilies. Cook for 5 minutes until well-cooked.
4. Add semolina and roast for 5 minutes. Turn off the flame.

5. Heat water in an idli steamer. Grease idli molds with oil.
6. Mix semolina mixture, drained tapioca pearls, coriander leaves, salt, and yogurt. Adjust consistency.
7. Pour batter into idli molds and steam for 15 minutes.
8. Serve hot.

Rava Idli with Foxtail Millet

Cooking time: 10 minutes
Servings: 3

Ingredients:
- 3 cups foxtail millet
- 1 cup dal
- ¼ tablespoon fenugreek seeds
- Oil
- Water
- Salt

Method:

1. Soak millet and dal separately in water for 6 hours. Soak fenugreek seeds with dal.
2. Grind dal and fenugreek seeds to a fine paste. Grind millet separately. Combine both batters.
3. Ferment batter overnight. Mix well.
4. Add salt and water to get the consistency of idli batter.
5. Grease idli plates with oil, steam for 10 minutes on medium-low heat.
6. Let it cool slightly, sprinkle with water, and remove hot idlis.
7. Adjust batter consistency with water for dosa. Heat a dosa tawa, pour

batter, spread, and cook. Serve hot.

Rava Dosa with Onions

Cooking Time: 15 minutes
Servings: 3 persons

Ingredients:
- 1/2 cup semolina (sooji)
- 2 teaspoons sliced coriander
- 1 sprig curry leaves, stripped
- 1/2 cup rice flour
- 1 tablespoon roughly minced ginger
- 1 sliced chili
- 1/4 cup Maida (all-purpose flour)
- 1 teaspoon cumin seeds
- 1 thinly sliced onion
- Ghee, as needed

Method:

1. Mix all the ingredients in a bowl except for onions, adding water until the batter is thin.
2. Set aside the onions. The batter should be very thin.
3. Heat a non-stick dosa plate. Drizzle a bit of ghee and pour the soupy batter, making a larger ring first and then filling in the middle.
4. Immediately sprinkle sliced onions on it. Add a teaspoon of oil/ghee. Cook on medium flame until the dosa turns golden.
5. Serve hot.

Buckwheat Dosa

Cooking Time: 10 minutes
Servings: 10 persons

Ingredients:
- 1 cup buckwheat flour
- 1/2 cup oat flour
- 1/2 cup almond flour
- Water, as needed
- 1/2 teaspoon salt

Method:

1. Whisk buckwheat, oat, and salted almond flours to prepare a smooth batter. Cover and let it ferment at room temperature overnight.
2. Add water to the batter as needed.
3. Heat a Dosa maker machine to setting 1.
4. Grease the upper and bottom cooking racks with a thin layer of oil. Pour spoonfuls of batter.
5. Cook for 3 minutes. Check the dosa and cook for an additional minute if necessary.
6. Serve hot.

Coriander Spinach Dosa

Cooking Time: 10 minutes
Servings: 5 persons

CHAPTER 03: BREAKFAST DELIGHTS OF INDIA

Ingredients:
- 2 1/2 cups rice (soaked overnight)
- 1 cup dal (soaked overnight)
- 1 tablespoon fenugreek seeds
- Salt, to taste
- Finely sliced spinach and coriander leaves
- Oil, for cooking

Method:

1. Wash rice, spinach, and coriander. Soak rice fully submerged in water for about six hours.
2. Soak dal and fenugreek seeds, ensuring they are fully submerged in water, for about six hours.
3. Grind soaked dal into a fluffy batter, adding only enough water to make it soft. The batter should be fluffy.
4. Crush the rice into a slightly smooth batter, adding only the necessary water. The rice batter can be a bit thicker, but it must be soft for the dosa batter.
5. Mix dal and rice batter, add salt, and let it ferment overnight. The batter will rise in volume.
6. Blend spinach leaves and coriander to create a smooth paste. Add this paste to the batter and mix well.
7. Heat a dosa tawa and pour a ladle of dosa batter. Spread it evenly in a clockwise direction from the center.
8. Add a few drops of oil around the edges and in the middle. Cook the dosa until it becomes golden brown at the bottom. Serve hot.

Aval Dosa

Cooking Time: 20 minutes
Servings: 4 persons

Ingredients:
- 3 cups rice
- 1 cup dal
- 2 teaspoons fenugreek seeds
- Salt
- Ghee or oil, as needed
- Water, as needed

Method:

1. Rinse rice and dal separately in water and cook them with enough salted water until soft.
2. Soak aval and add it to the washed rice with water.
3. Grind dal, rice mixture, and fenugreek seeds in a grinder until it becomes a smooth batter.
4. Preheat an oven to 180 degrees Celsius and turn it off.
5. Place the overnight batter in the oven.
6. Add salt to the batter the next day.
7. Heat a dosa tawa and pour a ladle of dosa batter.
8. Spread the batter evenly with a slotted spoon. Sprinkle the sides with some oil.
9. Cook until it turns golden.

Dadpe Pohe

Cooking Time: 30 minutes
Servings: 3 persons

Ingredients:
- 1 1/2 cups small flattened rice
- 1 cup thinly sliced onions
- 3/4 cup grated coconut
- 2 tablespoons powdered sugar
- 2-3 teaspoons lemon zest
- 3 teaspoons fresh peanuts
- 2 tablespoons coriander leaves
- Salt, to taste
- 3 teaspoons oil
- 1/4 teaspoon asafetida

Method:

1. Mix finely sliced onions, grated coconut, cinnamon, sugar, and lemon zest.
2. Spread flattened rice in a bowl and mix gently at the edges.
3. Heat a pan and add oil. Add fresh peanuts and fry until they change color. Remove and set aside.
4. Now add mustard seeds to the same hot oil. Add asafetida, chopped chilies, and curry leaves. Turn off the flame and add turmeric powder. Mix well.
5. Pour this mixture over the prepared pohe.
6. Give the whole mixture a quick stir.
7. Cover and let it rest for around 10 to 15 minutes to blend and absorb all the flavors.
8. Serve this tasty Dadpe Pohe for brunch or as a snack anytime.

Tomato and Peas Pohe

Cooking Time: 50 minutes
Servings: 3 persons

Ingredients:
- 2 teaspoons olive oil
- 1 large minced onion
- 1 clove of garlic, thinly minced
- 3 small-sized tomatoes, thinly sliced
- 1/2 cup sugar
- 1 teaspoon new oregano
- 1 cup water, or as needed
- 1 teaspoon tomato paste
- 1 small diced zucchini
- 1 cup peas
- Salt, to taste

Method:

1. Rinse poha with enough water and set aside for 10 minutes.
2. After 10 minutes, drain the water, fluff the poha, and separate any lumps, if any.

5

Chapter 4: Indian Lunch and Dinner Delights

In Indian cuisine, the main course meals are the heart of lunch and dinner gatherings. While dinners might be lighter, lunches are often hearty and elaborate. In this chapter, we present a diverse collection of recipes ideal for both lunch and dinner. Beyond just sharing recipes, this chapter aims to spark your culinary creativity, encouraging you to explore beyond these pages and experiment with a myriad of dishes. Here's a selection of dishes to elevate your lunch and dinner experiences.

Madras Style Chicken Curry

Serving: 4 people

Preparation Time: 2 hours

Ingredients:
- Ghee
- Onion
- Coriander
- Garlic
- Fresh Ginger
- Salt to taste

- Skinless boneless chicken thighs
- Citrus zest
- Sliced tomatoes
- Curry Powder
- Coconut milk

Instructions:

1) Heat a large pot over medium heat. Add sliced onions, chopped garlic, and crushed ginger in ghee. Stir until the onions are tender, about 10 minutes.

2) Add curry powder, salt, and chili powder. Cook until aromatic.

3) Increase the heat to medium, add coconut milk and tomatoes. Cook for a while.

4) Add sliced chicken pieces to the gravy, cover, and cook. Stir occasionally for 25 minutes.

5) To finish the sauce, add chopped coriander. Garnish with lemon zest before serving.

Casserole Chicken Tikka Masala

Serving: 4 people

Cooking Time: 3 hours

Ingredients:
- Eight chicken thighs with bone
- 1 tablespoon lime zest
- For Marinade:
- Crushed ginger
- Crushed garlic
- Yogurt as needed
- Pinch of chili powder

- 1 teaspoon coriander
- 1 teaspoon cumin
- 1 teaspoon garam masala
- 1 teaspoon turmeric
- Small chili
- For Sauce:
- 1 ½ tablespoons butter
- Large diced onion
- 1 tablespoon cumin seeds
- 1 tablespoon mustard seeds
- ½ teaspoon crushed fenugreek
- ½ teaspoon paprika
- 3 cardamom pods
- Large cinnamon slice
- 1 tablespoon tomato puree
- 40g chopped almonds
- 1 teaspoon vinegar
- Milk as needed
- Passata as needed

Instructions:

1) Cut chicken and marinate with lemon juice and salt. Let it sit while preparing the seasoning.

2) Blend ginger and garlic, setting aside a quarter of the paste. Add other marinade ingredients and blend to a paste.

3) Marinate chicken in the mixture for at least 4 hours.

4) Heat ghee in a deep pan over medium heat. Cook onions until browned.

5) Add spices and the reserved ginger-garlic paste. Cook for 5 minutes. Add tomato sauce, almonds, and vinegar. Heat for a while.

6) Add passata and water. Simmer for 2-3 hours until a thick sauce forms. It can be refrigerated for 24 hours.

7) Preheat the grill.

8) Grill chicken until charred and cooked. Remove from the oven.

9) Reheat the sauce, add reserved marinade and curry sauce to the chicken. Cook until done. Let it rest for a few minutes.

10) Garnish with cilantro and almonds, then serve.

Beef Kofta with Saag Aloo

Serving: 4 people

Cooking Time: 1 hour

Ingredients:
- 1 onion
- 1 garlic clove
- 2 small-medium potatoes
- Coriander
- ½ teaspoon cumin
- ½ teaspoon turmeric
- ½ teaspoon mustard
- Chicken stock
- 300g minced beef
- Coconut Milk as needed
- ½ teaspoon lemon zest
- Water

Instructions:
1) Chop onion, slice garlic, and cube potatoes. Chop coriander.
2) Heat oil in a pan over medium heat. Cook garlic and onion until tender. Set aside half of it.
3) Add rest of onion to the pan with cumin, turmeric, and mustard. Cook for 3 minutes.
4) Add potatoes, water, and half a pot of chicken stock. Cover and simmer

for 15-20 mins.

5) Mix beef with salt and black pepper. Form into small balls. Fry until golden brown.

6) Remove koftas from the pan.

7) Put koftas in the simmering mixture.

8) Add spinach, cover, and let it sit for 10 minutes. Stir in spinach. Sprinkle with lemon zest and serve.

Mango Chicken Curry

Serving: 4 people

Cooking Time: 2 hours

Ingredients:
- 2 teaspoons coconut oil
- 1 large onion, sliced
- 4 garlic cloves
- 8 teaspoons chopped ginger
- 4 teaspoons curry powder
- Salt and pepper, to taste
- 3 mangos, sliced and diced
- Coconut milk, as needed
- 2-4 chicken thighs, sliced

Instructions:

1) Heat coconut oil in a large deep pan over medium heat. Add sliced onion, garlic, and ginger. Cook until they turn brown.

2) Add curry powder, salt, pepper, 1 cup of fresh mangoes, and coconut milk. Mix well.

3) Pour the sauce into the pan, add chicken and ½ cup of water. Cover and

cook for 20 minutes. Reduce heat if the sauce starts sticking to the pan.

4) Add the remaining mango to the dish once the chicken is fully cooked. Serve.

Tandoori Curry Sandwich

Serving: 4 people

Cooking Time: 1 hour

Ingredients:
- 1 whole chicken, cut into pieces
- 1 cup Greek yogurt
- ½ yellow onion, diced
- 1 freshly grated ginger
- 2 garlic cloves
- 2 tablespoons citrus juice
- ½ teaspoon cumin
- ½ teaspoon ground cilantro
- 1 tablespoon olive oil
- Salt, to taste
- Potatoes
- For Sandwiches:
- Big whole wheat bread, half warmed
- Regular Greek yogurt
- ½ teaspoon cumin
- ½ teaspoon ground cilantro
- ¼ teaspoon garlic powder
- Salt, to taste
- Tomatoes
- Lettuce

Instructions:
1) Place chicken pieces in a large zip-lock bag.
2) Blend yogurt, onion, ginger, garlic, lemon juice, cumin, coriander, and oil until creamy. Season with salt and pepper.
3) Pour the sauce into the zip-lock bag with chicken. Marinate in the fridge for at least 4 hours.
4) Preheat the oven to 500 degrees. Place the chicken on a rack, skin side down. Roast for about 35 minutes until brown spots appear, flipping once. Reduce heat to 450 and continue to cook for about 10 more minutes until chicken is cooked through.
5) Dice the remaining chicken into bite-sized pieces if desired.
6) In a shallow bowl, mix yogurt and spices. Open each pita half to form a pocket and fill with chicken, lettuce, tomato, sauce, and yogurt.

Buttery Chicken Curry with Vegetables

Serving: 3 people

Cooking Time: 2 hours

Ingredients:
- 2 tablespoons butter
- 1 large white onion, finely diced
- 2 large garlic cloves
- 1 teaspoon fresh ginger
- 1 tablespoon Garam Masala
- 1 tablespoon curry powder
- 1 tablespoon cilantro powder
- ½ teaspoon paprika
- ¼ tablespoon cinnamon
- ¼ tablespoon chili flakes

- 2 tomatoes
- 1 400 ml bottle of coconut milk

Instructions:

1) Heat butter in a wide skillet or pot over medium-low heat until melted. Add onion and cook for about 6 minutes until translucent.

2) Add garlic and ginger, sauté until aromatic, about 5 minutes. Add garam masala, curry powder, cilantro, paprika, and cinnamon. Cook for about 1 minute, stirring occasionally.

3) Add chili flakes and tomatoes. Let the sauce boil for about 15 minutes until it thickens and becomes a deep red-brown color.

4) Remove from heat and blend in a mixer, adding salt and water if needed to reach desired consistency. Blend in batches if necessary.

5) Return the sauce to the pot. Add coconut milk and sugar. Add cooked lentils, tomatoes, chickpeas, and vegan chicken if desired. Cook for 10-15 minutes.

6) Serve garnished with corn and coriander.

Paneer Pulao

Serving: 4 people

Cooking Time: 2 hours

Ingredients:
- 1 cup Basmati rice
- 1 ½ cups paneer cubes
- ½ cup peas and carrots
- 1 large onion
- 2 green chilies
- 1 teaspoon ginger-garlic paste

- Coriander leaves, diced, as desired
- Salt, as required
- Oil or Ghee

Instructions:

1) Rinse and soak rice for 30 minutes. Heat ghee in a saucepan over medium heat for 3 minutes. Add drained rice and cook until dry.

2) Heat oil in a pan over medium heat. Add onion, green chili and fry until onion is translucent.

3) Add ginger-garlic paste, fry, then add vegetables. Fry until half-cooked.

4) Add 1 cup water and salt. Let it cook. Add cooked rice. Cover and cook over medium heat.

5) Prepare paneer cubes. Toast paneer in a non-stick skillet until golden.

6) Once the pulao is done, add drained paneer. Ensure paneer is water-free before adding. Serve.

Dal Makhani

Serving: 4 people

Cooking Time: 2 hours

Ingredients:
- 2 teaspoons red beans, soaked overnight
- 1 spoonful red chili powder
- 8 teaspoons butter
- 1 tall onion, chopped
- Half cup tomato puree
- Half cup fresh milk
- Half teaspoon ginger paste
- Salt, to taste

- 2 slices ginger, sliced
- 2 large green chilies, diced
- Half cup dal, soaked overnight
- 1/2 teaspoon garlic paste

Instructions:

1) Soak dal overnight in two cups of water. Drain and cook it in a pressure cooker with salt and 3 cups of water until tender.

2) Heat a pan over medium heat and add cumin seeds. Add ginger and garlic paste until cumin seeds crackle. Add carrots, sliced green chilies, and tomato puree.

3) Fry until the mixture turns golden. For an authentic Dal Makhani look, it's recommended to use ghee instead of oil.

4) Once the masala is cooked to your liking, add rajma and dal. Let it simmer.

5) Add garam masala and salt to taste. Bring to a boil, and add more water if the dal is too thick.

6) Finally, add fresh cream and mix well. This will make your dal creamy and flavorful.

Lemon Chicken

Serving: 4 people

Cooking Time: 2 hours

Ingredients:
- Four skinless chicken breasts
- One tablespoon lemon zest
- 1 tablespoon honey
- 1 cup oil
- 2 cloves garlic, minced

- 1 teaspoon crushed oregano
- Fresh green salad and potatoes, for serving

Instructions:

1) Preheat the oven to 170C. Place the chicken in a deep oven tray.

2) In a pan, combine all the ingredients and heat for 1 minute. Pour over the chicken.

3) Grill the chicken for 45 minutes, basting every 10 minutes. The juice will thicken, giving the chicken a glossy coating.

4) Let the chicken rest for 5 minutes before serving with a green salad and fresh potatoes.

Chettinad Trout Fry

Serving: 2 people

Cooking Time: 2 hours

Ingredients:
- 400g Fish
- 1 tablespoon turmeric powder
- Salt, to taste
- One tablespoon lemon juice
- 3 onions
- 2 garlic cloves
- 2 tablespoons ginger
- 2 teaspoons cumin seeds
- 2 teaspoons rice flour
- Oil, as needed
- 1 tablespoon red chili powder
- 1 tablespoon coriander powder

Instructions:
1) Cut the fish into pieces and wash them.
2) Marinate with turmeric powder, salt, and lemon juice. Set aside.
3) Blend cumin seeds, garlic, ginger, and onion into a paste.
4) Transfer the masala paste to a pan, add red chili powder, coriander powder, rice flour, salt, and 2 tablespoons of oil to make a thick paste.
5) Coat fish pieces evenly with the masala paste.
6) Heat oil in a grill pan or skillet. Fry fish pieces until cooked on one side, then turn.
7) Place the fried fish on a clean cloth to remove excess oil.
8) Serve with freshly boiled rice.

Mutton Do Pyaaza

Serving: 2 people

Cooking Time: 1 hour

Ingredients:
  - Half kilogram Mutton
  - Half cup yogurt
  - 3 Cardamom
  - 5 Chilies, to taste
  - Half teaspoon Cinnamon powder
  - Half teaspoon cumin
  - 1 tablespoon garlic paste
  - Salt, to taste
  - 1 teaspoon powdered red chili
  - Half tablespoon turmeric
  - Half cup Oil
  - 3 diced onions

- One teaspoon poppy seeds
- One teaspoon Coconut soil

Instructions:
1) Clean the beef and strain.
2) Mix yogurt, cardamom, cinnamon powder, chilies, cumin, garlic paste, salt, red chili powder, and turmeric.
3) Add the mixture to the meat and let it marinate for 1 hour.
4) Heat oil in a skillet, fry the onion until lightly browned. Remove onion, cook the meat in the same pan.
5) When yogurt water dries out, add enough water to cook the meat. Cover and cook until tender.
6) Add coconut and poppy seeds.
7) Add the fried onion and cook for 2 minutes. Serve.

Makhmali Kofte

Serving: 3 people

Cooking Time: 2 hours

Ingredients:
  For the Koftas:
  - 400g Indian Cottage Cheese (Paneer), sliced
  - 2 large baked and mashed potatoes
  - 2 chopped Green Chilies
  - ¼ teaspoon white pepper powder
  - Two broad tablespoons of corn flour
  - 4 tablespoons oil
  - Salt, to taste

CHAPTER 4: INDIAN LUNCH AND DINNER DELIGHTS

For the Gravy:

- Quarter cup of oil
- 2 moderate onions, sliced
- 1 tablespoon ginger
- Half garlic plant, sliced
- 20 cashews, soaked for 10 minutes
- 1 cup pureed tomatoes
- 1 dark cardamom
- 3 gray cardamom
- 1 Bay leaf
- 1 pinch of cinnamon
- Half teaspoon chili powder
- 2 teaspoons milk
- One teaspoon Kasuri methi (fenugreek)
- Salt, to taste

Instructions:

1) Combine all the ingredients for Koftas well and form them into balls.
2) Heat the oil and cook the Koftas until golden brown.
3) Reserve half of the chopped onion.
4) Fry the reserved onions until golden brown in hot oil.
5) Blend the remaining onions, ginger, garlic, and cashews into a fine paste.
6) Heat oil and add all garam masala, cardamom, garlic, bay leaf, and cinnamon.
7) Add the paste as the spices change color. Heat on high for 3 minutes.
8) Add fried onion and stir-fry for 5 minutes.
9) Add tomato puree, Kashmiri red chili, and salt. Add a glass of water and simmer for 20 minutes.
10) Gently add the cream and methi when the mixture cools down slightly.
11) Place the sauce in a deep bowl. Lower the koftas into the sauce one by one, avoiding them from stacking on top of each other.
12) Drizzle a little cream on top. Serve warm.

Pasta Masala

Serving: 3 people

Cooking Time: 1 hour

Ingredients:*
- 1 cup pasta, your choice
- 1 tablespoon olive oil
- 1 teaspoon cumin seeds
- 3 sliced garlic cloves
- 1 small sliced onion
- 3 thin diced tomatoes
- 1 tablespoon turmeric powder
- 1 teaspoon curry powder
- 1 tablespoon coriander powder
- Ground red chili, to taste
- Salt, to taste
- 1 cup water, or as needed

Instructions:
1) Set an electric pot to high stir fry mode. Add oil and let it heat.
2) Add garlic, onions, and cumin seeds. Cook for a while.
3) Now add the tomatoes and cook until tender. Add all the dry spices and salt.
4) Fry for one or two minutes.
5) Add pasta and water. Mix well, then turn off stir fry mode.
6) Set it to high mode for 7 minutes, ensuring the vent is in the sealing position. After 10 minutes, release it.
7) Serve as desired.

Garlic Mushrooms

Serving: 3 people

Cooking Time: 1 hour

Ingredients:
- 2 tablespoons butter
- 2 tablespoons oil
- Quarter cup finely sliced onion
- 1 cup Button Mushrooms
- 2 tablespoons finely ground garlic
- 2 tablespoons fresh parsley, thinly sliced
- Half teaspoon thyme, finely minced
- Half teaspoon oregano, finely chopped
- Red chili flakes, to taste

Instructions:
1) In a non-stick skillet, add oil and butter and cook over low to moderate heat.
2) Add onions and stir-fry for 3 minutes.
3) Add mushrooms and fry until lightly browned.
4) Add all the spices and stir and cook well.
5) Cook until flavorful with garlic. Be careful not to let the garlic burn.
6) Add the remaining parsley and turn off the heat gently. Enjoy.

6

Chapter 05: Indian Sweet Treat Recipes

Sweets serve as the perfect conclusion to any meal, acting like the icing on a plate. It's universally acknowledged that desserts provide a satisfying end to every dining experience. It's no surprise that people harbor a fondness for sweet treats. These delectable indulgences not only constitute an integral part of our daily diet but also find a place in various religious offerings. Across the board, sugar, milk, and khoya form the fundamental elements in the preparation of Indian desserts.

CHAPTER 05: INDIAN SWEET TREAT RECIPES

Shahi Falooda

Ingredients

- Two bottles of milk
- 2 tablespoons of rice
- Two tablespoons of honey
- Two teaspoons of flavored syrup
- Two tablespoons of finely minced dry fruits of your choice

Instructions

1. Cook the rice in water for about 15 minutes, then strain and set it aside.
2. In a blender, combine the milk, sugar, and dry fruits, and blend until it becomes creamy.
3. Divide the cooked rice into two glasses.
4. Pour half of the milk mixture into each glass. Mix well, add syrup, and chill in the refrigerator.
5. If you prefer, add a scoop of ice cream and garnish with dried berries. Serve with a long-handled spoon.

Gulab Jamun

Ingredients
- For the dough balls:
- 1 cup of condensed milk
- 110g plain flour
- 1.5 teaspoons of baking powder
- 0.5 teaspoon of baking soda
- 1.5 cups of milk
- 25g of warmed sugar
- Oil for frying
- For the syrup:
- 1 cup of caster sugar
- 100ml water
- Saffron to taste
- For garnishing:
- 1 tablespoon of sliced pistachio nuts
- 1 tablespoon of toasted almonds

Instructions

1. Combine all the dough ball ingredients in a bowl, adding enough water to form a smooth, sticky dough. Cover and let it rest for 20 minutes. Shape the dough into small round pieces.
2. Heat oil with high sides in a deep fryer. Fry the dough balls until they turn golden brown, then remove and drain on a serving plate.
3. Prepare a sugar syrup by boiling the sugar, water, and saffron.
4. Once the dough balls are cooked, add them to the sugar syrup and allow them to soak for about an hour.
5. Garnish with nuts and serve.

Kulfi

Ingredients
 - 1 liter of whole milk
 - Half a cup of heavy cream
 - 1/3 cup of crushed khoya
 - 1 tablespoon of dry milk powder
 - A combination of 3 tablespoons of cashews and pistachios
 - 10 teaspoons of sugar
 - 5 green cardamom pods, seeds separated and ground

Instructions

1. In a heavy-bottomed pan, heat the whole milk over low to medium heat.
2. Add the cream after about 10 minutes.
3. Let the mixture simmer and then reduce the heat to low.
4. Allow the milk to simmer for about 25 minutes on low heat, stirring constantly.

5. After 25-30 minutes, when the milk has thickened, add the crushed khoya and continue stirring until it melts, which takes about 10 minutes.
6. Once the khoya has melted, add the sugar and cook until it dissolves.
7. Add the finely chopped nuts.
8. Mix in the condensed milk and cook for an additional 5 minutes until it thickens further. It will thicken more as it cools.
9. Remove the pan from the heat, add the ground cardamom, and let it cool.
10. Pour the mixture into kulfi molds or your preferred container. Cover and freeze until fully set.
11. To remove the kulfi, place the mold under warm, running water and tap it on the counter. Enjoy the delicious Kulfi Malai.

Mishti Doi

Ingredients
- 1 liter of full cream milk
- 8 cardamom pods
- Curd to taste
- 1 cup of sugar, or to taste

Instructions

1. Heat one liter of full cream milk in a deep non-stick saucepan.
2. Stir continuously while heating the milk.
3. Add a cup of sugar and mix well.
4. Boil the milk over medium heat until it thickens, stirring occasionally until it reduces to half. Meanwhile, place two tablespoons of brown sugar in a saucepan, add water, and mix well. Heat over low flame until the sugar dissolves.
5. Transfer the caramelized sugar to the boiling milk.

6. Stir well and bring the milk to another simmer. Let it cool to room temperature.
7. Once the milk has cooled, transfer it to an earthen pot or another container of your choice.
8. Add a teaspoon of curd and mix well.
9. Cover and let it set for 8 hours in a warm place or until fully set.
10. Refrigerate for 2 hours for a creamy texture. Garnish with sliced nuts.
11. Serve chilled mishti doi.

Indian Cham Cham Dessert

Ingredients
   - Four cups of heavy cream milk
   - Paneer (prepared at home or store-bought)
   - Two cups of sugar
   - Five cups of water
   - 1/8 tsp cardamom powder

Instructions

1. Prepare the paneer first. Take a small piece of paneer and rub it between your fingertips to check if enough water has been extracted. After about 30 seconds of pressing, it should form a smooth yet firm surface.
2. Place the soaked paneer on a smooth surface and knead it for 3 to 4 minutes until it forms a smooth, soft dough. Add a teaspoon of water if the paneer is too crumbly.
3. Divide the paneer dough into eight equal portions and shape each into a flat oval disc.
4. For the syrup, bring 5 cups of water to a boil in a large saucepan. Add sugar and stir until fully dissolved. Use a wide pan as the Cham Cham

will expand as they cook in the syrup.
5. Add the paneer discs to the syrup and stir to coat them evenly. Reduce the heat to medium and cover with a lid. Cook for 15 minutes.
6. Uncover the pan, flip the Cham Chams, and cook for another 15 minutes. Check if the Cham Chams are firm yet spongy. Turn off the heat and let them sit for an additional 10 minutes.
7. Remove the Cham Chams from the syrup and allow them to cool. Serve chilled.

Sitaphal

Ingredients
- 1 cup of fresh custard apple pulp (seedless)
- 2 egg whites
- 400 ml of chilled cream milk
- 1/3 cup powdered sugar
- 1/3 teaspoon of vanilla extract

Instructions

1. Grind the custard apple pulp into a coarse paste using a blender.
2. While the Sitaphal is freezing, whisk the two egg whites in a dry container until they become frothy with stiff peaks using a hand beater. Be cautious to separate the egg white carefully, as even a small amount of yolk can prevent them from becoming stiff.
3. Mix the water, cream, and vanilla extract in a separate bowl. Avoid whisking too vigorously, as overwhisking will turn the cream into butter.
4. Add the custard apple pulp to the cream mixture and mix it thoroughly with a spoon.
5. Gently fold this mixture into the egg whites. The goal is to retain as

much air as possible in the egg whites to achieve a silky, smooth, and delicious ice cream. Once thoroughly combined, transfer it to a freezer-safe container.
6. Freeze for at least 3 hours

. Remove and stir it again in the freezer until smooth.
7. Return it to the freezer and let it set. Scoop into individual bowls or cups and serve.

Til Ladu (Sesame Seed Ladoo)

Ingredients
- 500g sesame seeds
- 1 liter milk or water
- 750g clarified butter (ghee)
- 750g sugar
- 3 cups of water
- 5-10 drops of orange food coloring
- 10-12 strands of saffron, soaked
- 50 cashews, chopped
- Raisins, as desired
- 12 cardamom pods, seeds removed and ground

Instructions

1. Prepare a thin batter with water and sesame seeds. Heat ghee in a pan.
2. Fill a frying pan or strainer with some of the batter.
3. Place it over the hot ghee and tap the strainer on the side of the pan to let tiny droplets fall into the ghee. The droplets should fall easily, forming small round shapes.

4. Fry the droplets until they turn golden brown. Use the remaining batter to form a thin layer over the fried sesame seeds.
5. Prepare a sugar syrup by boiling sugar and water until it forms a syrup of one and a half-thread consistency.
6. Add saffron water and food coloring to the syrup. Add the fried sesame seeds, cardamom, dried fruits, and honey. Mix well.
7. Allow it to rest for about 1.5 hours, occasionally adding a little hot water and covering it.
8. Shape the mixture into round balls using moist hands.

Peanut Indian Brittle

Ingredients
- 1 cup of roasted peanuts (skin removed)
- 1 cup of sugar

Instructions

1. Grind the peanuts into a fine powder using a blender.
2. Heat a pan over medium flame and add sugar and 2 tablespoons of water.
3. Stir continuously. The sugar will gradually caramelize.
4. Once all the lumps have melted and the sugar has turned golden brown, turn off the heat and add the peanut powder. Mix well and quickly transfer the mixture onto a flat tray.
5. While the mixture is still hot, use a knife to create lines on it. Let it cool.
6. Once cooled, cut along the lines to create squares.

Indian Barfi

Ingredients
- 2 cups of milk powder
- 300ml heavy cream
- 400g sweetened condensed milk
- 1/2 cup of finely sliced pistachios

Instructions

1. Combine milk and cream and whisk until creamy.
2. Cover the pan and microwave it for about 8 minutes.
3. Keep a close eye on the dish, and if it seems like it might boil over, stop the microwave for 8 to 10 seconds and then continue until the 8-minute mark. Take it out and mix well.
4. Return the pan to the microwave and set it for another 8 minutes on high. Monitor it carefully in the first minute and then allow the cooking to continue.
5. Sprinkle the sliced pistachios over the barfi's surface while still in the microwave and let it sit for 10 minutes.
6. Remove the barfi from the microwave after 10 minutes and cut it into 2-inch squares. Let it cool and then serve.

Indian Rice Pudding

Ingredients
- 1/2 cup of rice
- 3 cups of full-fat milk
- 1 cup of coconut milk

- 1/2 cup of sugar
- 1/2 teaspoon of ground green cardamom
- 1 tablespoon of oil
- 1 tablespoon of cashews
- 1 tablespoon of pistachios
- 1 tablespoon of almonds, chopped
- 1 teaspoon of saffron

Instructions

1. Soak the rice for 30 minutes to reduce the cooking time.
2. If using whole cardamom pods, coarsely crush them with a mortar and pestle. Add nuts and crush them into a fine paste.
3. In a deep saucepan, combine the milk, coconut milk, and rice. Bring it to a boil. Reduce the heat to simmer, add sugar and cardamom. Stir well.
4. Cook until the rice becomes tender and not rubbery, stirring regularly. The cooking time will vary, approximately 1 hour, depending on the rice used. Keep an eye on the mixture as it cooks, adding more sugar if necessary.
5. Prepare your desired toppings and toast the nuts in a pan.
6. Let it cool and then serve.

Jalebi

Ingredients
- 1 cup of flour
- 1 tablespoon of chickpea flour
- 1/4 teaspoon of cardamom powder
- 1/2 teaspoon of baking powder
- 1/4 teaspoon of baking soda

- 5 teaspoons of yogurt
- Orange food coloring (optional)
- Water, as needed
- Oil or ghee for frying
- For the syrup:
- 1 cup of sugar
- 1/2 cup of water
- 1/4 teaspoon of cardamom powder
- 1/2 teaspoon of lemon juice

Instructions

1. Mix all the ingredients to make a batter.
2. Aim for a thick consistency; add food color and water as needed.
3. The batter should not be too thick. Depending on the consistency of the flour and chickpea flour, you may need up to 3/4 cup of water.
4. Cover the batter and let it ferment for 10 hours.
5. Whisk the batter a bit more later. If the batter is too thick at this stage, add a little water.
6. Meanwhile, boil water and sugar for the syrup until it reaches a one and a half-thread consistency.
7. Set the batter aside.
8. Heat oil or ghee in a pan. Keep the heat on moderate-low.
9. Squeeze the batter into hot oil, allowing the spiral shape. Ensure you maintain the shape at low heat, otherwise, it may spread. If the batter disperses in the oil, it is likely too thin; add more flour.
10. Fry until crispy. Remove from the oil and immediately dip in warm sugar syrup for a few seconds on each side.
11. Remove from the syrup and place on a serving tray. Enjoy homemade jalebi with rabri or milk. You can garnish the top with almonds.

Shakkarpara

Ingredients
- 2 cups of all-purpose flour
- 1/4 cup of ghee
- 1 cup of sugar
- Ghee, for frying

Instructions

1. Begin by grinding the all-purpose flour to make the dough for shakarparas.
2. Mix all-purpose flour and 1/4 cup of melted ghee in a bowl. Mix well. Add water. In winters, use warm water to knead the flour. We used half a cup of water for this volume of dough. Cover the dough and let it rest for half an hour.
3. Then knead the dough again after 20 minutes to make it smoother and fluffier. Divide the dough into two parts. Keep one part covered to prevent drying. First, shape it into a flat dough disc.
4. Take out the sheet that has been kept aside. Flatten the rolled sheet from the edges. Then cut it into wide strips. Cut the strips into long pieces, adjusting the size as desired. Place the shakarparas separately on a tray. Repeat the process.
5. Heat oil enough to fry them. Drop a piece of shakarpara to check the temperature. Moderately hot ghee is needed for frying shakarparas. Keep the flame at medium-low. When the ghee is hot, drop the rest of the shakarparas into the ghee.
6. When the shakarparas rise to the top, flip them and fry until they become light golden from all sides. Remove the fried shakarparas on a plate. Keep the pan tilted on the edge of the wok so that the excess ghee flows back into the

CHAPTER 05: INDIAN SWEET TREAT RECIPES

wok.

7. Prepare a sugar syrup in another container. Add sugar and water to the mixture. Cook until the sugar dissolves. Take a few drops in a bowl to test, then take it between your thumb and index finger. Check if a long thread is formed as you move your fingers apart. The syrup is ready. Switch off the flame.

8. Place this vessel on a net stand so that the syrup thickens a bit. When the syrup becomes slightly dense in consistency, drop the shakarparas into the sugar syrup and coat them well. Directly transfer the shakarparas from the syrup into a large bowl after mixing them in the syrup. Pour out the excess syrup from the same bowl. Reheat it slightly if the syrup becomes too thick while coating the shakarparas.

9. Stir gently to separate the sugar-coated shakarparas; otherwise, they may stick together.

Enjoy your delicious homemade Indian sweets!

7

Chapter 06: Vegetarian Indian Delights

In recent times, an increasing number of individuals are embracing vegetarian cuisine over non-vegetarian options. This shift is primarily driven by health considerations, as many non-vegetarian dishes tend to increase the fat content in our bodies and can be slower to digest. These dietary choices are influenced by various health concerns, including issues such as obesity, thyroid imbalances, and weight gain. In this chapter, we will explore a variety of vegetarian dishes that are not only delicious but also packed with essential nutrients to promote overall well-being.

CHAPTER 06: VEGETARIAN INDIAN DELIGHTS

Vegetable Biryani

Servings: 3

Cooking Time: 2 hours

Ingredients:
   - 2 teaspoons of oil
   - One small cauliflower, broken into small florets

- 2 large sweet potatoes, peeled and cubed
- 1 large onion, chopped
- One stock of hot veggies
- One tablespoon of curry paste
- One chili, thinly sliced
- A big pinch of saffron threads
- One tablespoon of mustard seeds
- 500 g Rice
- 140 g beans
- Two tablespoons of lemon juice
- A handful of coriander leaves

Steps:

1) Heat oil in a large deep pan over medium heat. Add onions and sauté for about 5 minutes until softened. Add mustard seeds; cook until they start popping, about 5 more minutes.

2) Stir in ginger-garlic paste, onions, and ½ cup of water. Bring to a boil and cook for 5 minutes until water is absorbed. Add peas, onions, and carrots. Add all the spices. Stir gently, cover, and simmer for three minutes.

3) Add 4 cups of water and bring to a boil over medium heat. Add rice, reduce heat to low, cover, and cook for 10 minutes. Reduce heat further and continue to cook for another 20 minutes until rice is tender.

Indian Sparkling Dal

Servings: 4

Cooking Time: 1 hour

Ingredients:
- One tablespoon of oil

- 1 cup sliced onion
- 2 garlic cloves, finely sliced
- One tablespoon diced ginger
- 4 cups of water
- 1 cup rinsed dried red lentils
- One tablespoon cumin
- One tablespoon of coriander
- One tablespoon of turmeric
- ¼ teaspoon cardamom
- ¼ teaspoon cinnamon
- ¼ teaspoon pepper
- Salt, to taste
- 2 tablespoons of tomato paste

Steps:

1) Heat oil in a medium soup pan over medium heat. Add onion, garlic, and ginger. Cook, stirring regularly, for about 6 minutes.

2) Add water, lentils, vegetables and salt. Stir continuously. Bring to a gentle boil, then reduce heat, cover, and cook for about 20 minutes or until lentils are very soft.

3) Stir in tomato paste and cook for a few more minutes. Serve and enjoy.

Cabbage Curry

Servings: 4

Cooking Time: 2 hours

Ingredients:
- 3 tablespoons of cooking oil
- 2 dried hot chili peppers, chopped

- 1 tablespoon black split skinned lentils
- 1 tablespoon Bengal gram
- 1 teaspoon mustard seeds
- A few curry leaves
- A pinch of asafetida powder
- 4 green chili peppers, chopped
- 1 cabbage head, thinly sliced
- ¼ cup frozen peas
- Grated coconut, 2 tablespoons

Steps:

1) Heat oil in a large skillet over medium-high heat. Add dried chili peppers, lentils, and mustard seeds. When the lentils start browning, add curry leaves and asafetida powder. Stir well.

2) Add green chili peppers and cook for another 3 minutes.

3) Add cabbage, peas, and lentils. Season with salt. Cook until it begins to wilt but still retains some crunch, about 10 minutes.

4) Add coconut, simmer for another 2 minutes. Serve immediately.

Indian Spinach Dal

Servings: 4

Cooking Time: 2 hours

Ingredients:
- 2 cups of yellow split peas
- 8 cups of water
- 2 teaspoons of freshly squeezed lemon juice
- 2 teaspoons of kosher salt
- 8 teaspoons of unsalted butter

- 2 teaspoons of cumin seeds
- 1 ½ teaspoons of turmeric
- 5 large garlic cloves, minced
- ¼ cup fresh ginger, peeled and finely chopped
- 1 medium serrano chili, stemmed and thinly chopped
- 8 ounces spinach, washed and coarsely chopped

Steps:

1) Rinse split peas under cold water in a fine-mesh strainer. Transfer to a large saucepan, add water, and bring to a boil. Reduce heat to medium-low and simmer, stirring occasionally until peas are completely soft, about 30 minutes.

2) Remove from heat, add lemon juice and salt.

3) Heat butter in a frying pan over medium heat until foamy. Add cumin seeds and turmeric; cook until fragrant, about 3 minutes.

4) Add garlic, ginger, and serrano chili; season with salt. Cook for 2-3 minutes until vegetables are soft. Add spinach and cook until wilted, about 4 minutes.

5) Combine spinach mixture with cooked split peas. Serve with steamed rice or naan.

Masoor Dal

Servings: 4

Cooking Time: 2 hours

Ingredients:
- 2 cups of dry masoor dal, sorted and rinsed
- 8 cups of water
- 1 tablespoon of oil (coconut oil or neutral flavored)

- 1 large yellow onion, finely diced
- 6 cloves of garlic, minced
- 1 tablespoon of minced ginger
- 2 green chilies, minced
- 1 tablespoon of Indian curry powder
- 1 teaspoon of whole mustard seeds
- 1 teaspoon of coriander
- ½ teaspoon of cumin
- 1 ½ teaspoon salt, or to taste
- 1 ½ cups of fresh chopped tomatoes

Steps:

1) In a large pot, combine lentils and water. Bring to a boil, then reduce heat to simmer. Cook partially covered until lentils are soft, about 15-20 minutes.

2) In a skillet, heat oil over medium heat. Add a pinch of salt, onion, garlic, ginger, and chilies. Fry for about 5 minutes until tender.

3) Add spices including salt, curry powder, mustard, coriander, and cumin. Cook for 60 seconds, then add tomatoes. Cook for about 7 minutes until tomatoes are soft and saucy.

4) Add tadka to cooked lentils, simmer over low heat for about 5 minutes.

5) Garnish with basmati rice and cilantro. Serve and enjoy.

8

Conclusion

Indian cuisine is indeed a diverse and exciting world of flavors and ingredients. It offers a wide range of dishes, from mild and comforting to spicy and bold, making it suitable for various taste preferences. While Indian cooking might seem daunting at first due to its extensive use of spices and unique ingredients, it can be an incredibly rewarding culinary journey.

Here are some key points to keep in mind when exploring Indian cuisine at home:

1. Understand the Basics: Start by familiarizing yourself with the core spices and ingredients used in Indian cooking. Common spices include cumin, coriander, turmeric, garam masala, and fenugreek. Each spice adds a unique flavor to the dishes.

2. Experiment Gradually: Don't be afraid to experiment with Indian recipes, but start slowly. Begin with simpler dishes and gradually work your way up to more complex ones. This will help you build confidence in handling spices and flavors.

3. Balancing Flavors: Indian cuisine is all about achieving a balance of flavors - sweet, sour, salty, bitter, and umami. Spices play a crucial role in achieving this

balance. Taste your dishes as you cook, and adjust the seasonings accordingly.

4. Cooking Techniques: Indian cuisine includes a variety of cooking techniques, including sautéing, frying, roasting, and simmering. Different dishes may require different methods, so pay attention to the instructions in your recipes.

5. Regional Diversity: India is a vast country with diverse culinary traditions. Different regions have their own specialties and ingredients. Explore dishes from various regions to experience the full range of Indian flavors.

6. Vegetarian-Friendly: Indian cuisine offers a wide array of vegetarian and vegan dishes. It's a great choice for those who prefer plant-based meals. Vegetables, legumes, and dairy products are often featured in Indian cooking.

7. Oil and Fat: Indian cooking typically uses various types of cooking fats, including ghee, mustard oil, and coconut oil. Understanding the appropriate use of these fats can greatly impact the flavor of your dishes.

8. Fresh Ingredients: Whenever possible, use fresh and high-quality ingredients. Fresh spices, herbs, and vegetables will enhance the flavor of your dishes.

9. Online Resources: There are numerous websites, cookbooks, and YouTube channels dedicated to Indian cooking. These resources can provide step-by-step guidance and tips for specific dishes.

10. Enjoy the Journey: Cooking Indian food at home can be a delightful and educational experience. Don't get discouraged by the complexity of some dishes. Take your time, enjoy the process, and savor the delicious results.

Indian cuisine is a beautiful fusion of flavors and aromas. As you gain more experience, you'll become more comfortable with the spices and techniques, and you'll be able to create authentic and delightful Indian dishes at home.

www.ingramcontent.com/pod-product-compliance
Lightning Source LLC
LaVergne TN
LVHW020429080526
838202LV00055B/5096